CLAN LINE Il
PHOTOGRAPHS

The First 40 Years 1878 - 1918

an publication

Published by:- Avid Publications,
Garth Boulevard
Bebington,
Wirral,
Merseyside. UK
CH63 5LS
Telephone / Fax: (44) 0151 645 2047
e-mail info @ avidpublications.co.uk
website http//www.avidpublications.co.uk

CLAN LINE IN PHOTOGRAPHS - THE FIRST 40 YEARS, 1878 - 1918
by TONY BLACKLER
ISBN 1 902964 3 3 0 © Tony Blackler 2002
A CIP record for this book is available from the British Library
Front Cover: An unusal view of Clan Mackenzie *in wartime 'dazzle' paint. (see page 87)*
Rear Cover: Clan Ferguson . *'Turret' Construction clearly visible. (see Page 13)*

**OTHER BOOKS AND VIDEOS ARE AVAILBLE DIRECT FROM AVID
PUBLICATIONS ARE DETAILED AT THE REAR OF THIS BOOK**

INTRODUCTION

It is almost a quarter of a century since the Centenary of the founding, in 1878 by Charles Cayzer, of what was to become, in 1890, Clan Line Steamers Ltd. Since then practically all of the ships with the familiar two red bands on a black funnel have disappeared from the oceans along with the company, but they are not forgotten. Clan Line is still very much spoken about in today's shipping circles. Many of the senior officials in ports and in the shipping industry worldwide have fond memories of the company and its ships. As far as I am aware there has been no definitive history written about the whole company, generally known throughout the last century as Cayzer Irvine & Co. Ltd. This volume of old photographs compiled from the collections of Bob Briscoe and myself (both of us ex company employees) will, I hope, go some way to revive old memories.

Charles Cayzer grew up in Victorian times when Britain had a vast empire that needed to be served by people and trade. It was a time of huge change in the shipping industry with steam ships taking over from sail, the opening of the Suez Canal and later the Panama Canal. Trade routes and transport times underwent massive restructuring. It was a time when Britain had many entrepreneurial men who had great ideas about opening up world trade. Men like Arthur Anderson of the Peninsular and Oriental Line, (P&O), Alfred Holt of Blue Funnel fame and of course, Charles Cayzer, along with many more, setting out to build huge fleets of fast and in those days, modern ships.

Charles William Cayzer was brought up near the River Thames in London, although his ancestors came from Cornwall. Therefore he knew about ships from an early age. In his teens he took a job as a shipmaster's clerk on a sailing ship and from that day until he died a millionaire in 1916, ships and shipping were his life. At the age of 17, in 1861, Charles Cayzer was working in a Bombay shipping office. This firm later became a part of the British India Steam Navigation Co. Ltd. swallowed up in the 20th century by P&O. It may have been this association that led Charles Cayzer to have two red bands on his ships' funnels in place of British India's two white ones. There was always a close rivalry between the two companies as their trade routes were often very similar. Indeed, company folklore stated that Charles Cayzer once vowed that he would have twice as many red bands on the oceans as there were white ones.

In 1878 a company known as Cayzer Irvine & Co. became the managing owners for Cayzer's ships. The Irvine was from Cayzer's partnership with Captain Alexander Irvine, a former British India Master whom he had known for many years. The first ship to be built was the Clan Alpine by Alexander Stephen at Glasgow. Unfortunately, Captain Irvine died early in 1879 at the age of 44, but the company's name never changed. From his main office in Liverpool, Cayzer set up an office in Glasgow which quickly became the head office. From the start, all his ships were registered at that port. Exceptions were those that came from other companies, by purchase or wartime management. Over the years the Cayzer empire expanded and in due course he absorbed other companies into his. It is because of this that we see ships with other funnel colours with Clan names and Clan Line funnel colours on ships belonging to other companies in the group. These types of associations continued to the final days and were often linked to trading areas or specific routes. This book provides several examples of how the ships and their colours were interchanged.

In 1894 Cayzer Irvine & Co. acquired the Persian Gulf Steamship Company and its four ships. This was done with a view to entering the Persian Gulf trade. During 1918 Houston Line (British & South American Steam Navigation Company) was acquired and so was the Scottish Shire Line, with the South American and Australian trade rights of these companies. At the end of the Company's first 40 years the fleet stood at a total of 86 steamships. The routes covered India, South Africa, South America and Australia.

By the spring of 1916 Sir Charles Cayzer, as he now was, having been knighted in 1897, was in a poor state of health and the losses of his ships in the War made matters worse. In all, 28 Clan ships and nearly 300 company lives were lost in the War. Charles Cayzer died on September 28th 1916, aged 73. Three of his sons took over the running of the company in accordance with their father's wishes, Lt. Cdr. August Cayzer R.N, became the Chairman.

At this point another era in the company's history starts. There was a massive rebuilding of the fleet after World War I, a feat repeated after World War II. Finally, the great names of Clan, Houston, Shire and many other associated companies ended in 1981 with the sale of Clan Line's last ship, the Clan Macgregor. My wife and I have fond memories of her. She was the only Clan ship that my wife was able to step foot on, albeit briefly, exactly one year before the end. However, it was a few more years before the final disappearance of all the ships and remaining parts of the empire that was started by Charles Cayzer in 1878.

©Tony Blackler 2002

ACKNOWLEDGEMENTS & FURTHER INFORMATION

If it had not been for the photographs taken and collected by Bob Briscoe and his idea of publishing his collection this work may never have been produced. To his collection I have added my own and I then pondered over how to put them in a logical order. I eventually concluded that they should not be in the same order that many fleet histories use; that of the date upon first entering a company's service. I decided to use the chronological order of the Official Number (O.N.) assigned to the ships upon entering the British Register. As most ships were registered originally in Glasgow, that allows the reader to follow the developments in ship design over a century. This order does not always work, as those ships acquired from abroad, bought from other companies or wartime managed may have Official Numbers issued by ports other than Glasgow, so the sequence is not always true to date of build or acquisition.

This book contains a number of photographs of ships which are described as 'turret deck'. I think a few paragraphs explaining the meaning of these terms and the reasons as to why this type of ship were built are needed as their strange appearance may leave the reader wondering.

The turret ship was created about the turn of the 19th century when steam ships had become firmly established. At this time a large range of new designs were built, each with its own peculiarities, advantages and disadvantages. The turret ship was a modification of an earlier American design known as the 'Whaleback' which had a much rounder hull form. The 'turret ship', or 'turret deck ship' as it is sometimes known, involved having a rounded sheer strake at the weather deck, then placing well inboard of that another part of the hull and more deck with the hatch covers inset from the edge of that deck, It formed a continuous 'trunk' on which the winch platforms, mast and accommodation were placed and it improved seaworthiness and stability by increasing the vessels reserve buoyancy. However, there could be stability problems if the ship was not loaded correctly or the double bottom tanks not ballasted, This, of course, is the case with most ships, even today. The 'turret' also had the effect of keeping heavy seas off the hatch covers. The system also had the advantages of acting as a feeder hopper when carrying bulk cargoes thus reducing the need for expensive shifting boards.

One of the greatest advantages to the shipowner was the fact that this design lowered the tonnage of the ship, yet she could carry more cargo. Thus, the shipowner earned more on freight and paid less port charges. Another spinoff was the fact that Suez Canal dues were at that time paid on the breadth of the ship at the upper dock. The turret being narrow at the upper deck, i.e. at the hatch cover level, meant that the Canal dues were reduced.

The turret ship design came from the William Doxford yard at Sunderland where most of these ships were built, although some were built under licence elsewhere. Initially, there was opposition to the design, but in 1891 Doxfords formed the Turret Steamship Company Ltd. to build a prototype appropriately named TURRET. This was delivered to the new company in 1892 and managed by Petersen, Tate & Co. of Newcastle-upon-Tyne. Several other vessels then followed and in 1896 the IMPERIALIST, renamed CLAN SHAW (1) and BULLIONIST (not renamed by Clan Line) were built. These two ships played an important part in the future of the design as they were sold to Cayzer Irvine & Co. Ltd. The company tried them out, found them to be satisfactory and ordered five more, but larger ships.

In all, 28 turret ships were built for Cayzer Irvine & Co. Ltd., better known as Clan Line Steamers. The big advantage to Clan Line was the reduction in Suez Canal dues, as most of their ships transited the Canal on their voyages to the Indian Ocean. Doxford's eventually completed a total of 176 turret ships and six more were built under licence by Swan Hunter, two by Vickers and one by Hawthorn Leslie. Most were fitted with Doxford engines.

From 1907 the changes that had been made to Tonnage Regulations and Load Line Regulations favoured the shelter deck type of ship rather than the turret ship, which meant the end of the turret ship building programme and the rise of the shelter deck design, that lasted until about the time Clan Line's last ship was built in 1967. Indeed, the turret ships were so well built that the last survivor was wrecked in 1983.

Much of the above information has been gleaned from The World Ship Society's publication of 1975, 'The Doxford Turret Ships' by Leonard Gray and John Lingwood. There is much more detailed information in that book with a complete list and history of all the 'turret ships' built.

In compiling this record of Clan Line ships I wish to acknowledge the invaluable works already in print of the following authors and publications:

Merchant Fleets in Profile (various volumes, principally No. 33) by Duncan Haws.

A Victorian Shipowner (a biography of Charles Cayzer produced for the Clan Line Centenary dinner in 1978) by Augustus Muir and Mair Davies, (published by Cayzer, Irvine & Co. Ltd.)

Clan Line in the Great War by Archibald Hurd, 1924, (published by Cassell & Co.)

In Danger's Hour by Gordon Holman, 1948, (published by Hodder & Stoughton Ltd.)

Mercantile Navy Lists, many years' editions held in the Guildhall Library, London.

Lloyd's Register of Ships, many years' editions held in Southampton Central Library, Warsash Maritime Centre Library and my own volumes.

British Vessels Lost at Sea 1914 - 18, HMSO 1919, (reprint published by Patrick Stephens 1979).

British Vessels Lost at Sea 1939 - 45, HMSO 1947, (reprint published by Patrick Stephens 1976).

Clan Line 1878 - 1978 by T. J. Culpin. (A thesis lodged in the library of Warsash Maritime Centre, formerly the School of Navigation, Southampton).

Scrap & Build, D.C.E. Burrell (published by the World Ship Society.)

For the later ships not included in this volume: Marine News, Journals of the World Ship Society. Sea Breezes, 1919 to the present. Personal records, Tony Blackler.

I would also like to express my particular thanks to Mr Alex Duncan as well as the World Ship Society (P.O. Box 706, Gravesend, Kent. DA12 5UB) for their permission to use important photographs that were outside my own and Bob Briscoe's collections.

NOTES AND ABBREVIATIONS

Signal letters of many ships changed from 1932 hence some ships are given two sets of signal letters by which all ships are identified by radio and flags.

Gross and net tonnages (grt & nrt) are those given for the ship shortly after her first survey. These figures may change considerably and frequently during the life of a ship. They indicate the volumetric size of a ship: 1 ton = 100 cubic feet of space.

Dimensions are generally registered length (between perpendiculars), extreme breadth and moulded depth. These figures are in feet and tenths of feet. They may change over time as ship measurement rules change. After World War 2 length overall is the length usually quoted.

The Summer draught, where given, is the amount of ship under water when she is fully loaded to the Summer loadline.

The engine details are given for engines as built. Over a period of years engines may be modified and re-rated in terms of power. Power terms also change over the years, as do the methods of calculation. The size of cylinders and the stroke of the pistons usually stayed the same. During this period many ship's engines were changed from coal to oil. This also affected specifications. After 1957 engine sizes were given in metric measurements and the Nominal Horse Power (NHP) was omitted from the registers.

I have included the builder's yard numbers, where known, as I know many ship enthusiasts like to be given this number as it provides an additional identification and reference for the ship. Like the Official Number (O.N.) it is unique, but unlike the O.N. it cannot be changed. The O.N. will often change with a change of flag.

Occasionally, an item of data is not available in the usual sources and where this occurs a ? is inserted against the heading.

A potted history is given before details of the disposal of all ships. The dates and events are not fully documented here due to space restrictions. Readers may find that some stories catch their attention and these may be followed up in other publications; many of which are mentioned in the previous list, but official records, if available, may contain more detail.

'Clan Lamont' 2090 tons. A typical early steamer built for Clan Line.

CLAN LINE IN PHOTOGRAPHS

Name	**CLAN BUCHANAN (l)**
Ex Names	
Official Number	85927
Signal letters	WJFV
GRT as built	2933
NRT	1913
Dimensions in feet	330.3 x 40.1 x 26.3
Summer Draught ?	
Built by	A. MacMillan & Son
Year	1882/2
At	Dumbarton
Yard number	237
Engine type	Compound inverted 2 cylinder steam, 39", 75" - Stroke 40"
NHP	400
Built by	D. Rowan & Co.
At	Glasgow

History

Iron built.

1900, approx.: engines tripled, 24fi", 40", 67" – Stroke 48" by Vickers, Sons & Maxim Ltd. Barrow-in-Furness. NHP now 360.

1904: sold to Essajee Tajbhoy, Bombay, India (later Shah S. N. Co. of India Ltd.). Renamed **SHAH ALLUM.**

Disposal

1909, June 10: wrecked at Piram, Cogho, India.

Photo credit   Blackler Collection (A Duncan)

Name	**CLAN CAMPBELL (ll)**
Ex Names	
Official Number	104576
Signal letters	NMRH
GRT as built	2600
NRT	1662
Dimensions in feet	312.0 x 40.2 x 24.7
Summer Draught	22' 7"
Built by	Naval Construction & Armament Co. Ltd.
Year	1894/10
At	Barrow-in-Furness
Yard number	228
Engine type	T3 23", 38", 63" - Stroke 42"
NHP	317
Built by	Naval Construction & Armament Co. Ltd.
At	Barrow-in-Furness

History

1913: sold to the Adelaide S. S. Co. Ltd. Renamed **CAMIRA**.

1925: owned by Ci Extrême Orientale, Shanghai, China. Renamed **YUNG NING**.

1927: renamed **COMMANDANT HENRI RIVIERE**.

1936: sold to Shiu Tsing Hong, China.

Disposal

1941, December: bombed at Canton, China, by Japanese aircraft.

Photo credit   Blackler collection (A. Duncan).

Name	**CLAN MENZIES (I)**
Ex Names	
Official Number	105979
Signal letters	PFGS
GRT as built	2669
NRT	1693
Dimensions in feet	312.3 x 40.2 x 23.5 Turret deck.
Summer Draught	22' 9"
Built by	Naval Construction & Armament Co. Ltd.
Year	1896/2
At	Barrow-in-Furness
Yard number	245
Engine type	T3 23", 38", 63" - Stroke 42"
NHP	317
Built by	Naval Construction & Armament Co. Ltd.
At	Barrow-in-Furness

History

1925: sold to A. Ardito, Genoa, Italy. Renamed **NOSTRA SIGNORA DI CORONATA.**

1901, May: first ship to take tea out of Chittagong, India, as the railway from Assam had been newly opened.

Disposal

1928: broken up in Italy.

Photo credit   Briscoe collection.

Name	**CLAN SUTHERLAND (l)**
Ex Names	
Official Number	106037
Signal letters	PMGJ
GRT as built	2820
NRT	1794
Dimensions in feet	326.0 x 40.2 x 23.5
Summer Draught	22' 8"
Built by	Naval Construction & Armaments Co. Ltd.
Year	1896/10
At	Barrow-in-Furness
Yard number	252
Engine type	T3 23", 38", 63" - Stroke 42"
NHP	317
Built by	Naval Construction & Armaments Co., Ltd.
At	Barrow-in-Furness

History

1917, April 17: damaged by a torpedo from a submarine off Start Point, Devon. Beached at Dartmouth, repaired at Falmouth. 12 killed.

1921: sold to T. Sato & Co., Dairen, Japan. Renamed **SHINSHU MARU**.

1925: sold to Azuma Kishen Goshi Kaisha, Dairen, Japan, but retained name.

Disposal

1933: broken up in Japan.

Photo credit   Blackler collection (A. Duncan)

Name	**CLAN MACDONALD (ll)**
Ex Names	
Official Number	106067
Signal letters	PQMD
GRT as built	4839
NRT	3113
Dimensions in feet	400.6 x 50.2 x 27.7 Turret deck
Summer Draught ?	
Built by	Wm. Doxford & Sons
Year	1897
At	Sunderland
Yard number	250
Engine type	T3 $27\frac{1}{2}$", $45\frac{1}{2}$", 75" - Stroke 54"
NHP	413
Built by	Wm. Doxford & Sons Ltd.
At	Sunderland

History

1922: sold to Hokuyo Kisen Goshi Kaisya, Dairen, Japan. Renamed **HOKUYO MARU**.

Disposal

1925: broken up in Japan.

Photo credit   Blackler collection (A. Duncan + Nautical Photo Agency)

Name	**CLAN FERGUSON (l)**
Ex Names	
Official Number	108779
Signal letters	QMDB
GRT as built	4808
NRT	3107
Dimensions in feet	400.6 x 50.2 x 27.5
Summer Draught ?	
Built by	Vickers, Sons & Maxim Ltd
Year	1898
At	Barrow-in-Furness
Yard number	267
Engine type	T3 27½", 45½", 75" - Stroke 54"
NHP	413
Built by	Vickers, Sons & Maxim Ltd.
At	Barrow-in-Furness
History	

Sister of **CLAN MACDONALD (ll).**

Disposal

1917, September 6: torpedoed by submarine off Morocco, sank in 7 minutes and 10 crew were lost. The 63 survivors were picked up and landed at Gibraltar.

Photo credit   Blackler collection (A Duncan)

Name	**CLAN CUMMING (l)**
Ex Names	
Official Number	108797
Signal letters	QTHS
GRT as built	4808
NRT	3108
Dimensions in feet	400.6 x 50.2 x 27.5
Summer Draught	?
Built by	Vickers, Sons & Maxim Ltd.
Year	1899
At	Barrow-in-Furness
Yard number	268
Engine type	T3 27½", 45½", 75" - Stroke 54"
NHP	413
Built by	Vickers, Sons & Maxim Ltd.
At	Barrow-in-Furness

History   Sister to **CLAN MACDONALD (l)** and **CLAN FERGUSON (l)**.

1917, November 5: torpedoed 20 miles from the Lizard, Cornwall. Towed to Falmouth, patched and sent to Liverpool. 15 dead.

1925: sold to Soc. Anon. Cantieri Olivio, Genoa, Italy. Renamed **ETTORE**.

1927: sold to Soc. Anon. Tito Campanella, Genoa, Italy. Renamed **ELISA CAMPANELLA**.

Disposal

1932: broken up at Genoa, Italy.

Photo credit   Blackler collection (WSS Photo Library)

15

Name	**CLAN MACAULAY (l)**
Ex Names	
Official Number	108800
Signal letters	RBGS
GRT as built	2834
NRT	1775
Dimensions in feet	326.0 x 40.2 x 23.6
Summer Draught	22' 2"
Built by	A. Stephen & Sons
Year	1899/4
At	Linthouse, Glasgow
Yard number	381
Engine type	T3 23", 38", 63" - Stroke 42"
NHP	313
Built by	A. Stephens & Sons
At	Glasgow

History

1915, September: requisitioned by the Government as a store carrier for the British Expeditionary Forces in France.

1917: returned to Clan Line.

Disposal

1929: broken up at Alloa, Scotland.

Photo credit   Blackler collection (WSS photo Library)

Name	**CLAN COLQUHOUN (I)**
Ex Names	
Official Number	111187
Signal letters	RCQD
GRT as built	5856
NRT	3760
Dimensions in feet	440.0 x 51.6 x 28.9 Turret deck.
Summer Draught	?
Built by	Wm. Doxford & Sons Ltd.
Year	1899
At	Sunderland
Yard number	269
Engine type	T3 27$\frac{1}{2}$", 45$\frac{1}{2}$", 75" – Stroke 60"
NHP	436
Built by	Wm. Doxford & Sons Ltd.
At	Sunderland

History

1916, 25 November: attacked by submarine **U 38,** using gunfire in the Mediterranean. Saved by her return gunfire.

1925: sold to Villain & Fassio, Genoa, Italy. Renamed **NASCO**.

1927: sold to Corado Soc. Anon. Di Nav, Genoa, Italy. Renamed **CENGIO**.

Disposal

1930: broken up in Italy.

Photo credit   Briscoe collection.

Name	**CLAN FARQUHAR (l)**
Ex Names	
Official Number	111209
Signal letters	RGSF
GRT as built	5858
NRT	3757
Dimensions in feet	439.0 x 51.6 x 28.9 Turret deck.
Summer Draught ?	
Built by	Wm. Doxford & Sons Ltd.
Year	1899
At	Sunderland
Yard number	271
Engine type	T3 27$\frac{1}{2}$", 45$\frac{1}{2}$", 75" - Stroke 60"
NHP	436
Built by	Wm. Doxford & Sons Ltd.
At	Sunderland
History	

Disposal

1917, February 26: torpedoed by a submarine 80 miles north of Benghazi, Libya. 49 lost.
24 survivors rescued by **HMS VERBENA** and landed at Malta.
The 2nd Engineer was taken prisoner and held in Austria.

Photo credit   Blackler collection (WSS Photo Library)

Name	**CLAN LAMONT (ll)**
Ex Names	
Official Number	111280
Signal letters	RTCJ
GRT as built	3594
NRT	2286
Dimensions in feet	355.0 x 45.6 x 24.7
Summer Draught ?	
Built by	Wm. Doxford & Sons Ltd.
Year	1900
At	Sunderland
Yard number	278
Engine type	T3 25¹/₂", 42", 69", - Stroke 48"
NHP	330
Built by	Wm. Doxford & Sons Ltd.
At	Sunderland

History

1914: almost the last vessel to leave Antwerp before the Germans captured the port. She left with a large number of refugees on board.

Disposal

1928, December: sold to P. & W. MacLellan, Bo'ness, Scotland, and broken up.

Photo credit   Blackler collection (A. Duncan)

Name	**CLAN STUART (ll)**
Ex Names	
Official Number	113911
Signal letters	RWLD
GRT as built	3594
NRT	2285
Dimensions in feet	355.0 x 45.6 x 24.7
Summer Draught	?
Built by	Wm. Doxford & Sons Ltd.
Year	1900
At	Sunderland
Yard number	280
Engine type	T3 25½", 42", 69" - Stroke 48"
NHP	330
Built by	Wm. Doxford & Sons Ltd.
At	Sunderland

History

1914: became a Government transport.

Disposal

1914, November 21: wrecked in Simons Bay, South Africa.

Photo credit   Blackler collection (Illustration from Shipping World July 1901)

Name	**HYPATIA**
Ex Names	
Official Number	115246
Signal letters	TFQM
GRT as built	5728
NRT	3549
Dimensions in feet	452.0 x 52.2 x 28.3
Summer Draught	26' 8"
Built by	Palmer's Shipbuilding & Iron Co., Ltd.
Year	1902/1
At	Newcastle-upon-Tyne
Yard number	760
Engine type	T3 30¹/₄", 50", 81¹/₂ - Stroke 54"
NHP	642
Built by	Palmer's Shipbuilding & Iron Co., Ltd.
At	Newcastle-upon-Tyne

History

Sister of **HYACINTHUS**.

1917, June 2: attacked by submarine in the Atlantic. The torpedo missed.

Disposal

1929, October 29: wrecked off Robben Island, Table Bay, South Africa.

Photo credit   Briscoe collection.

Name	**HYACINTHUS**
Ex Names	
Official Number	115279
Signal letters	TJMF
GRT as built	5756
NRT	3674
Dimensions in feet	452.0 x 52.2 x 28.3
Summer Draught	26' 8"
Built by	Palmer Bros. & Co.
Year	1902
At	Newcastle-upon-Tyne
Yard number	761
Engine type	T3 $30^{1}/_{4}$", 50", $81^{1}/_{2}$ - Stroke 54"
NHP	642
Built by	Palmer's Shipbuilding & Iron Works Co., Ltd.
At	Newcastle-upon-Tyne

History

Sister of **HYPATIA**.

1914: used as Army transport in the Mediterranean.

1917, April 4: attacked by a submarine off N W Ireland. The torpedo missed.

1917, December 25: a bad Christmas Day! Torpedoed in the English Channel by a submarine but reached port.

Disposal

1930: October, broken up in The Netherlands.

Photo credit   Briscoe collection.

Name	**CLAN LINDSAY (ll)**
Ex Names	
Official Number	115704
Signal letters	TPND
GRT as built	3935
NRT	2499
Dimensions in feet	360.2 x 48.1 x 24.5 Turret deck.
Summer Draught ?	
Built by	Wm. Doxford & Sons Ltd.
Year	1902
At	Sunderland
Yard number	299
Engine type	T3 25$^{1}/_{2}$", 42", 69" - Stroke 48"
NHP	330
Built by	Wm. Doxford & Sons Ltd.
Year	?
At	Sunderland
History	

1916, May 3: attacked by gunfire from a submarine in the Bay of Biscay.

Disposal
1931: broken up at Inverkeithing, Fife, Scotland, by Thomas W. Ward.

Photo credit   Blackler collection (WSPL)

Name	**CLAN CHATTAN (l)**
Ex Names	
Official Number	115711
Signal letters	TQTH
GRT as built	3938
NRT	2500
Dimensions in feet	359.8 x 48.1 x 24.4 Turret deck
Summer Draught ?	
Built by	Wm. Doxford & Sons Ltd.
Year	1902
At	Sunderland
Yard number	300
Engine type	T3 25½", 42", 69" - Stroke 48"
NHP	330
Built by	Wm. Doxford & Sons Ltd.
At	Sunderland
History	

Sister of **CLAN LINDSAY (l).**

Disposal

1930: broken up by P. & W. MacLellan, Bo'ness, Scotland.

Photo credit   Blackler collection (A. Duncan)

Name	**CLAN MACKINNON (ll)**
Ex Names	
Official Number	115746
Signal letters	TVMD
GRT as built	4788
NRT	3049
Dimensions in feet	395.4 x 50.9 x 27.0
Summer Draught	24' 1"
Built by	Wm. Denny & Bros.
Year	1903/3
At	Dumbarton
Yard number	675
Engine type	T3 26 $^5/_8$", 43", 71" - Stroke 60"
NHP	447
Built by	Wm. Denny & Bros.
At	Dumbarton

History

1927: sold to Lars Krogius, Helsinki, Finland, and renamed **HERAKLES**.

Disposal

1936, April 27: arrived at Bo'ness, Scotland, for scrapping by P. & W. MacLellan Ltd.

Photo credit   Briscoe collection.

Name	**CLAN MACLEOD (lll)**
Ex Names	
Official Number	115783
Signal letters	VFKT
GRT as built	4796
NRT	3043
Dimensions in feet	395.5 x 51.1 x 27.1
Summer Draught	?
Built by	Furness, Withy & Co. Ltd.
Year	1903/9
At	West Hartlepool
Yard number	267
Engine type	T3 26", 43", 71" - Stroke 48"
NHP	452
Built by	Richardsons, Westgarth & Co. Ltd.
At	Hartlepool

History

Disposal

1915, December 1: sunk by gunfire from a submarine in the Mediterranean, 80 miles ESE of Malta. 12 killed.

Photo credit   Blackler collection (A. Duncan)

Name	**CLAN MACINTOSH (ll)**
Ex Names	
Official Number	121290
Signal letters	HFLJ
GRT as built	4774
NRT	3043
Dimensions in feet	400.0 x 51.0 x 27.2
Summer Draught	24' 6"
Built by	Furness Withy & Co. Ltd
Year	1906/1
At	West Hartlepool
Yard number	288
Engine type	T3 26", 43", 71" - Stroke 48"
NHP	448
Built by	Richardsons, Westgarth & Co. Ltd.
At	West Hartlepool

History

1917, July 5: attacked by submarine **UC 71**, using gunfire in the Bristol Channel. Saved by her return gunfire.

Disposal

1932, May: sold to Smith & Houston at Port Glasgow, Scotland, for scrap.

Photo credit   Briscoe collection & Blackler collection (A. Duncan)

Name	**CLAN SINCLAIR (ll)**
Ex Names	
Official Number	124222
Signal letters	HLMT
GRT as built	5215
NRT	3291
Dimensions in feet	400.1 x 52.1 x 27.5 Turret deck
Summer Draught	24' 6"
Built by	Wm. Doxford & Sons Ltd.
Year	1907
At	Sunderland
Yard number	333
Engine type	T3 27½", 45½", 75" – Stroke 54"
NHP	413
Built by	Wm. Doxford & Sons Ltd.
At	Sunderland

History

Sister of **CLAN BUCHANAN (ll)**.

1917, April 18: attacked in the North Atlantic by a submarine using a torpedo which missed then gunfire which was returned. One shell apparently hit the submarine which dived, not to be seen again by the **CLAN SINCLAIR**.

Disposal

1933: broken up by Hughes Bolckow at Blyth, Northumberland.

Photo credit   Blackler collection (A. Duncan).

Name	**CLAN BUCHANAN (ll)**
Ex Names	
Official Number	124232
Signal letters	HLQT
GRT as built	5212
NRT	3288
Dimensions in feet	400.1 x 52.1 x 27.4 Turret Deck
Summer Draught	24' 6"
Built by	Wm. Doxford & Sons Ltd.
Year	1907
At	Sunderland
Yard number	335
Engine type	T3 27½", 45½", 75" - Stroke 54"
NHP	413
Built by	Wm. Doxford & Sons Ltd.
At	Sunderland

History

Clan Line's last turret ship. Sister to **CLAN SINCLAIR** (ll).

1916, November 12: attacked by submarine **U 49**, using gunfire off Cape Ortegal, Spain. Saved by her return gunfire.

Disposal

1933: broken up by at Blyth, Northumberland, by Hughes Bolckow.

Photo credit   Briscoe collection.

43

Name	**CLAN KENNETH (l)**
Ex Names	**ARDGRYFF** - 1918
Official Number	127551
Signal letters	HPRL
GRT as built	4897
NRT	3159
Dimensions in feet	400.0 x 52.0 x 27.4
Summer Draught	24" 5"
Built by	Russell & Co. Ltd.
Year	1909/9
At	Port Glasgow
Yard number	588
Engine type	T3 27", 44", 73" - Stroke 48"
NHP	479
Built by	Rankin & Blackmore Ltd.
At	Greenock

History

Built as **ARDGRYFF** for Lang & Fulton, Greenock.
1918: acquired by Cayzer Irvine & Co.

Disposal

1934: broken up at Blyth, Northumberland, by Hughes Bolckow.

Photo credit   Briscoe collection.

Name	**CLAN MACPHEE**
Ex Names	
Official Number	129578
Signal letters	HDWM/GQLR
GRT as built	5177
NRT	3225
Dimensions in feet	430.7 x 53.5 x 26.4
Summer Draught ?	
Built by	Irvine Shipbuilding & Drydock Co. Ltd.
Year	1911
At	West Hartlepool
Yard number	499
Engine type	T3 29", 49", 80" - Stroke 60"
NHP	497
Built by	Richardsons, Westgarth & Co. Ltd.
At	West Hartlepool

History

She once sailed from Fremantle, Australia, to Calais, France, with a cargo of wool in 30 days.

Disposal

1940, August 16: torpedoed by submarine **U 30** in Lat. 57° 30'N Long. 17° 14'W, 67 crew lost, (30+ in a lifeboat accident), 41 were rescued. Voyage from Liverpool, UK, to Bombay, India. The rescuing ship was the Hungarian **KELET**. She was torpedoed and sunk two days later. Only 18 members of the **CLAN MACPHEE**'s crew survived both sinkings. (The last sentence was given to me 1st hand by a survivor, Capt. Molyneux, in April 2001).

Photo credit   Briscoe collection & Blackler collection

BRITISH CARGO LINER TORPEDOED

17/8/40

ATTACK OFF HEBRIDES.

New York, Friday.—Mackay Radio reports that the British steamer Clan Macphee (6,628 tons) was torpedoed at 6.17 a.m. to-day, when about 700 miles west of the Hebrides on the Northern shipping lane.

The Clan Macphee is a cargo liner owned by the Clan Line, Limited, Glasgow. — Press Association War Special.

Name	**CLAN URQUHART (ll)**
Ex Names	**ARGYLLSHIRE (l)** - 1933
Official Number	129581
Signal letters	HTBG/GNZK
GRT as built	11949
NRT	7526
Dimensions in feet	526.2 x 61.4 x 33.3
Summer Draught	29' 11¾"
Built by	John Brown & Co. Ltd.
Year	1911/6
At	Clydebank
Yard number	399
Engine type	Q4 x 2 25", 35½", 51", 72", - Stroke 51"
NHP	1,264
Built by	John Brown & Co. Ltd.
At	Clydebank
History	

Launched as **ARGYLLSHIRE** for Scottish Shire Line, and taken over in 1917, with the company, (Turnbull, Martin & Co.) by Cayzer Irvine & Co. Ltd.

1915, May 27: attacked by a submarine in the English Channel. Two torpedoes missed.

1917, February 5: attacked and torpedoed by a submarine off Start Point, Devon, UK. Made port.

1933: renamed by Clan Line.

Disposal

1937: fire broke out during scrapping at Briton Ferry, Wales.

Photo credit   Briscoe collection.

Name	**CLAN MACGILLIVRAY (l)**
Ex Names	
Official Number	129596
Signal letters	HTJC/GQLC
GRT as built	5023
NRT	3107
Dimensions in feet	430.6 x 53.6 x 26.6
Summer Draught	24" 5"
Built by	Sir W. G. Armstrong Whitworth & Co. Ltd.
Year	1911
At	Newcastle-upon-Tyne
Yard number	834
Engine type	T3 29", 49", 80" - Stroke 60"
NHP	496
Built by	Wallsend Slipway Co. Ltd.
At	Newcastle-upon-Tyne

History

1915: took 1250 troops to Gallipoli, Turkey, from Australia, then she became a hospital ship, and troopship in the Mediterranean.

1948, October: sold to the Eastern Asia Navigation Co., Hong Kong, and renamed **MACLOCK**. This ship survived both World Wars unscathed.

Disposal

1949, Jan 1: arrived at Bruges, Belgium, for scrapping.

Photo credit   Briscoe collection & Blackler collection

50

Name	**CLAN GRAHAM (lll)**
Ex Names	**PORT LINCOLN** – 1927 **CAMBRIAN BARONESS** - 1929
Official Number	132733
Signal letters	HWFD/GKRT
GRT as built	7243
NRT	4638
Dimensions in feet	426.0 x 54.1 x 29.3
Summer Draught	27' 6"
Built by	Hawthorn, Leslie & Co., Ltd.
Year	1912/6
At	Newcastle-upon-Tyne
Yard number	502
Engine type	Q4 $26^{3}/_{4}$", 39", 56", $81^{1}/_{2}$" - Stroke 54"
NHP	777
Built by	North East Marine Engineering Co., Ltd.
At	Newcastle-upon-Tyne

History   1912: launched as **PORT LINCOLN** for William Milburn & Co.

1914: transferred to Commonwealth & Dominion Line upon its formation.

1927: sold to Wm. Thomas Shipping Co., London. Renamed **CAMBRIAN BARONESS**.

1929: sold to Cayzer Irvine & Co. Ltd. Renamed **CLAN GRAHAM**.

1935: transferred to Houston Line. Retained name.

1938: sold to Neil & Pandelis Ltd., London. Renamed **MARITIMA**.

Disposal

1942: November 2: torpedoed by a submarine in Lat. 52° 20'N Long. 45° 40'W . (About 500 miles North East of St. Johns, Newfoundland).

Photo credit   Blackler collection. A. Duncan & WSPL

Name	**CLAN ROBERTSON (ll)**
Ex Names	**OTAKI** - 1934
Official Number	132763
Signal letters	?/GCLN
GRT as built	7964
NRT	4985
Dimensions in feet	449.1 x 58.2 x 37.1
Summer Draught	29' 3"
Built by	Barclay, Curle & Co. Ltd.
Year	1920/2 **At** Glasgow
Yard number	574
Engine type	T3 x 2 26½", 44", 73" - Stroke 48"
NHP	1122
Built by	Barclay, Curle & Co., Ltd. **At** Glasgow

History Sister of **CLAN COLQUHOUN** (ll). N.B. This ship's Official number is not in sequence as she was registered first at Plymouth which was using an older numerical sequence.
1919: launched as the **WAR JUPITER** for the Shipping Controller.
1920: entered service as the **OTAKI** for New Zealand Shipping Co., Ltd.
1934 acquired by Cayzer Irvine & Co., Ltd. Renamed **CLAN ROBERTSON** (ll)
1938 sold to J. A. Billmeir, (Stanhope S. S. Co. Ltd.). Renamed **STANFLEET.**
1939: sold to Zubi Shipping Co., London, (a Blue Star subsidiary). Renamed **PACIFIC STAR.**
Disposal
1942, October 27: torpedoed near the Canary Islands.
1942, October 28: ship abandoned as she was taking in water. 100 people on board were rescued.
1942, October 30: she sank in heavy weather.
Photo credit   Blackler collection

Name	**BUTESHIRE**
Ex Names	**CLAN MACEWEN** - 1920
Official Number	133053
Signal letters	HWCR/GNZP
GRT as built	6544
NRT	4162
Dimensions in feet	430.5 X 53.6 X 26.6
Summer Draught	27' 2$^{1}/_{2}$"
Built by	Palmer's Shipbuilding & Iron Co., Ltd.
Year	1912
At	Newcastle-upon-Tyne
Yard number	817
Engine type	T3 29", 49", 80" - Stroke 60"
NHP	496
Built by	Palmer's Shipbuilding & Iron Co., Ltd.
At	Newcastle-upon-Tyne

History

1915: served in the Dardenelles Campaign, Turkey, in a variety of capacities.

1920: transferred to the Scottish Shire Line and renamed by Cayzer Irvine & Co., Ltd.

1932: transferred to Houston Line (London) Ltd. Retained name.

1939 – 45: served unscathed during the Second World War.

Disposal

1948, February 25: arrived at Preston, Lancashire, for scrapping by Thomas Ward.

Photo credit   Briscoe collection

Name	**BERWICKSHIRE**
Ex Names	**CLAN MACARTHUR (II)** – 1920
Official Number	133085
Signal letters	JBHF/GNZL
GRT as built	7382
NRT	4679
Dimensions in feet	450.1 x 57.1 x 28.6
Summer Draught	?
Built by	Sir W. G. Armstrong Whitworth & Co., Ltd.
Year	1912
At	Newcastle-upon-Tyne
Yard number	346
Engine type	T3 31½", 52", 86" - Stroke 60"
NHP	574
Built by	Wallsend Slipway Co., Ltd.
At	Newcastle-upon-Tyne

History

The largest ship yet built for Clan Line.

1917, April 27: chased by a submarine off the Isles of Scilly. Escaped by using her speed.

1920: transferred to Scottish Shire Line.

Disposal

1944, August 20: torpedoed by a submarine in Lat. 30° 58'S Long. 38° 50'W, off South Africa. She was on a voyage from Durban, South Africa, to Tamatave, Madagascar, and Port Louis, Mauritius. The 94 survivors were rescued by **HMS NORWICH CITY**. 8 lives were lost.

Photo credit   Briscoe collection.

Name	**CLAN MACBRIDE (l)**
Ex Names	
Official Number	133087
Signal letters	JHBS/GQLV
GRT as built	4886
NRT	3009
Dimensions in feet	390.0 x 50.5 x 27.9
Summer Draught	24' 11"
Built by	Ropner Shipbuilding & Repair Co., (Stockton), Ltd.
Year	1912/13
At	Stockton-on-Tees
Yard number	474
Engine type	T3 26", 43", 71" - Stroke 48"
NHP	393
Built by	Blair & Co., Ltd.
At	Stockton - on - Tees

History

1936: sold to McGowan & Gross Ltd., London, for £37,000 (with **CLAN MACKELLAR (l)**) and renamed **HEATHCOT**.

Disposal

1938: sold to shipbreakers at Osaka, Japan.

Photo credit	Briscoe collection.

Name	**CLAN MACKELLAR (l)**
Ex Names	**HARFLETE** – launched as
Official Number	133105
Signal letters	JBSC/GFBS
GRT as built	4925
NRT	3062
Dimensions in feet	410.2 x 52.0 x 27.9
Summer Draught	28' 2"
Built by	Northumberland Shipbuilding Co., Ltd.
Year	1913/3
At	Newcastle-upon-Tyne
Yard number	208
Engine type	T3 28", 46½", 78" - Stroke 54"
NHP	501
Built by	Earle's Co., Ltd.
At	Hull

History

1912: launched as **HARFLETE** for J. & C. Harrison, London.

1913: purchased during fitting out by Cayzer Irvine & Co., Ltd. Renamed **CLAN MACKELLAR**.

1914 -18: used as a transport for the Indian Government.

1936: sold with **CLAN MACBRIDE (l)** to MacGowan & Gross Ltd., London, for £37,000, and renamed **MOORCOT**.

Disposal

1938: sold to shipbreakers at Osaka, Japan.

Photo credit   Briscoe collection & Blackler collection

62

Name	**CLAN MACBETH (l)**
Ex Names	
Official Number	133120
Signal letters	JCGV/GQLN
GRT as built	4650
NRT	2881
Dimensions in feet	385.0 x 51.7 x 27.4
Summer Draught	24' 9"
Built by	Sir J. Laing & Sons Ltd.
Year	1913/5
At	Sunderland
Yard number	640
Engine type	T3 25½", 42", 70" - Stroke 48"
NHP	394
Built by	Richardsons, Westgarth & Co., Ltd.
At	West Hartlepool

History

1937: sold to Nailsea Steamship Co., Ltd., Cardiff, for £16,250. Renamed **NAILSEA VALE**.

Disposal

1938: Sold to Arnott & Young & Co., (Shipbreaking) Ltd., Dalmuir, for £11,000 and scrapped.

Photo credit   Briscoe collection & Blackler collection

Name	**CLAN MACQUARRIE**
Ex Names	
Official Number	133157
Signal letters	JDHL/GQLB
GRT as built	6430
NRT	4083
Dimensions in feet	429.2 x 53.7 x 26.6
Summer Draught	?
Built by	Alexander Stephen & Son Ltd.
Year	1913
At	Glasgow
Yard number	456
Engine type	T3 29", 49", 80" - Stroke 60"
NHP	496
Built by	Alexander Stephen & Son Ltd.
At	Glasgow

History

1914 – 1917: taken over by the Admiralty and used as a stores and ammunition carrier.

Disposal

1942, June 13: torpedoed and gunned by a submarine in Lat. 5° 30'N Long. 23° 30'W, (over 600 miles from Freetown, Sierra Leone). She was on a voyage from Durban, South Africa, to New York, USA. The crew set off in 3 boats and only one person was lost.

Photo credit   Briscoe collection & Blackler collection

Name	**CLAN GRANT (lll)**
Ex Names	**PORT MACQUARRIE** - 1927 **CAMBRIAN MARCHIONESS** - 1929
Official Number	135132
Signal letters	HWPC/GKXM
GRT as built	7236
NRT	4638
Dimensions in feet	426.0 x 54.1 x 29.3
Summer Draught	27' 7$^{1}/_{4}$"
Built by	Hawthorn, Leslie & Co., Ltd.
Year	1912/9
At	Newcastle-upon-Tyne
Yard number	456
Engine type	Q4 26$^{3}/_{4}$", 39", 56", 81$^{1}/_{2}$" - Stroke 54"
NHP	777
Built by	North East Marine Engineering Co., Ltd.
At	Newcastle-upon-Tyne

History   Sister of **CLAN GRAHAM** (111).

1912: launched as **PORT MACQUARRIE** for Anglo-Australian S. N. Co., Ltd. (Wm. Milburn).

1914: transferred to the Commonwealth & Dominion Line.

1927: sold with her sister to R. J. Thomas. Renamed **CAMBRIAN MARCHIONESS**.

1929: Sold to Cayzer Irvine & Co., Ltd. Renamed **CLAN GRANT**.

1935: transferred to Houston Line. Retained name.

1939: sold to Stanhope Shipping Co., London (J. Billmeir). Renamed **STANGRANT**.

Disposal

1940, October 13: torpedoed by a submarine in Lat. 58° 27'N Long. 12° 36'W (west of Isle of Lewis, Scotland). 8 lives lost.

Photo credit   Blackler collection (WSPL)

Name	**CLAN ROSS (ll)**
Ex Names	
Official Number	136330
Signal letters	JHBM/GQLD
GRT as built	5971
NRT	3757
Dimensions in feet	430.0 x 54.3 x 29.4
Summer Draught	?
Built by	Swan, Hunter & Wigham Richardson Ltd.
Year	1914
At	Newcastle-upon-Tyne
Yard number	959
Engine type	T3 27½", 54½", 75" - Stroke 54"
NHP	413
Built by	Swan, Hunter & Wigham Richardson Ltd.
At	Newcastle-upon-Tyne

History

1918, May 5: torpedoed by submarine in the Mediterranean. She reached port (Toulon, France) after a huge salvage operation by the ship's officers and the French Navy, but 9 crew were lost.

1938: transferred to Houston Line, retained name.

1940, June 24: damaged by bombs from an aircraft in Lat. 43° 54'N Long. 1° 53'W.

Disposal

1942, April 2: torpedoed and sunk by a submarine in Lat. 15° 58'N Long. 68° 24'E. (Indian Ocean). 11 lost their lives. Two boats made for India, One was picked up by a Norwegian ship and the other boat's crew was rescued by a native craft 50 miles off the Indian coast.

Photo credit   Briscoe collection & Blackler collection

Name	**CLAN KEITH (1)**
Ex Names	**ETONIAN** - 1918
Official Number	136654
Signal letters	JFGB/GFNW
GRT as built	4306
NRT	2685
Dimensions in feet	385.0 x 52.0 x 25.1
Summer Draught	24' 8"
Built by	Bartram & Sons, Ltd.
Year	1914/3
At	Sunderland
Yard number	231
Engine type	T3 26", 43", 71" - Stroke 48"
NHP	401
Built by	J.Dickinson & Sons, Ltd.
At	Sunderland

History

1914: launched as **ETONIAN** for J. Mathias, Cardiff, (Cambrian S. N. Co., Ltd.)

1918: sold to Cayzer Irvine & Co., Ltd. Renamed **CLAN KEITH**.

1920: transferred to Houston Line. Renamed **HILARIUS**.

1924: Reverted to **CLAN KEITH**.

1937: sold to Minster S. S. Co., London. Renamed **ORMINSTER**.

1940: Acquired by South American Saint Line. Name retained owing to wartime restrictions on name changes.

Disposal

1944, August 25: Torpedoed off Cap d'Antifer, France, 6 killed but 57 rescued.

Photo credit   Blackler collection (WSPL).

72

Name	**CLAN MACKAY (IV)**
Ex Names	**SÜDMARK** – 1914 **HUNTSCRAFT** - 1921
Official Number	136793
Signal letters	JKGF/GQMX
GRT as built	5113
NRT	3176
Dimensions in feet	420.0 x 54.1 x 26.3
Summer Draught	25' 6"
Built by	Wm. Doxford & Sons Ltd.
Year	1913/7
At	Sunderland
Yard number	455
Engine type	T3 27", 44$\frac{1}{2}$", 75" - Stroke 54"
NHP	577
Built by	Wm. Doxford & Sons Ltd.
At	Sunderland

History

1913: launched as **SÜDMARK** for the Hamburg South America Line, Germany.

1914: taken as a prize by the British and transferred to the Shipping Controller. Renamed **HUNTSCRAFT** and managed by Harris & Dixon Ltd.

1917: management transferred to the Union-Castle Mail S. S. Co. Ltd., London.

1919: acquired by Cayzer Irvine & Co., Ltd. Retained name until name change restrictions were lifted in 1921, then renamed **CLAN MACKAY**.

Disposal

1934: wrecked on passage from Australia to Canada, on Carpenters Rocks, Sierra Leone.

Photo credit   Blackler collection & A. Duncan)

Name	**CLAN OGILVY (ll)**
Ex Names	
Official Number	137782
Signal letters	JLHQ/GQLF
GRT as built	5909
NRT	3716
Dimensions in feet	430.0 x 54.2 x 29.4
Summer Draught	?
Built by	Wm. Doxford & Sons Ltd.
Year	1914
At	Sunderland
Yard number	470
Engine type	T3 27$\frac{1}{2}$", 45$\frac{1}{2}$", 75" - Stroke 54"
NHP	413
Built by	Wm. Doxford & Sons Ltd.
At	Sunderland

History

1938: transferred to Houston Line. Retained name.

1940, June 30: damaged by a torpedo from a submarine, in the Bay of Biscay, Lat. 46° 17'N Long. 14° 35'W. Made port in a badly damaged condition.

Disposal   1941, March 20: torpedoed and sunk by a submarine, near the Cape Verde Islands in Lat. 20° 04'N Long. 25° 45'W, on a voyage from Freetown, Sierra Leone, to the UK. 26 of the crew lost their lives in various ways before being repatriated. The stories of these survivors is a long one.

I recently met one (Capt. John Chapple) in April 2001. He recalled the 16 days he was in a lifeboat and told me that he was torpedoed four times during WW2!

Photo credit   Briscoe collection & Blackler collection

Name	**CLAN MACBRAYNE (l)**
Ex Names	
Official Number	137811
Signal letters	JMNR/ GQLY
GRT as built	4818
NRT	2978
Dimensions in feet	390.0 x 50.5 x 28.0
Summer Draught	24' 10"
Built by	Ropner & Sons Ltd.
Year	1916/4
At	Stockton - on - Tees
Yard number	504
Engine type	T3 26", 43", 71" - Stroke 48"
NHP	403
Built by	Blair & Co., Ltd.
At	Stockton - on - Tees

History

1943: transferred to Houston Line. Retained name.

1948: sold to C. Galanos, Panama. Renamed **SAN GIORGIO**.

Disposal

1950: broken up by Thos. W. Ward, at Barrow-in-Furness.

Photo credit   Briscoe collection & Blackler collection (B. & A. Fielden)

Name	**CLAN STUART (lll)**
Ex Names	
Official Number	137827
Signal letters	JNKS/GQLZ
GRT as built	5775
NRT	3639
Dimensions in feet	423.5 x 56.0 x 28.7
Summer Draught	25' 5"
Built by	Russell & Co.
Year	1916/10
At	Port Glasgow
Yard number	689
Engine type	T3 27", 44", 73" - Stroke 48"
NHP	538
Built by	J. G. Kincaid & Co., Ltd.
At	Greenock

History

1916, Dec 22: attacked by submarine in the Mediterranean. The torpedo missed.

Disposal

1940, March 3: sunk in collision with an unknown vessel, in convoy, in fog, off Start Point, South Devon, England. All the crew were saved by a French trawler, **NOTRE DAME DE MONTLIGNON**, and landed at Plymouth.

Photo credit Briscoe collection & Blackler collection

BRITISH STEAMER SUNK IN COLLISION

The Clan Line steamer **Clan Stuart** (5,760 tons) foundered in the Channel last night after colliding with another vessel.

Lifeboats went out in response to an S O S and all the crew of 75 were saved.

Name	**CLAN RANALD (lll)**
Ex Names	
Official Number	137833
Signal letters	JPBD/GQMF
GRT as built	5503
NRT	3446
Dimensions in feet	409.1 x 54.0 x 28.9
Summer Draught	25' 6"
Built by	Napier & Miller Ltd.
Year	1917/3
At	Glasgow
Yard number	199
Engine type	T3 27", 44", 73" - Stroke 48"
NHP	538
Built by	J. G. Kincaid & Co., Ltd.
At	Greenock

History

1943: transferred to Houston Line. Retained name.

1947: sold to Pace Bros., Valletta, Malta, renamed **VALLETTA CITY**.

1951: sold to Pala & Franceschini, Italy, renamed **VALLETTA**.

Disposal

1958: scrapped at La Spezia, Italy.

Photo credit   Briscoe collection & Blackler collection (B. & A Fielden)

Name	**CLAN MALCOLM (I)**
Ex Names	
Official Number	137837
Signal letters	JPFW/GQMB
GRT as built	5994
NRT	3724
Dimensions in feet	405.1 x 53.3 x 33.5
Summer Draught	27' 5"
Built by	Craig, Taylor & Co., Ltd.
Year	1917
At	Stockton-on-Tees
Yard number	172
Engine type	T3 28", 46", 75" - Stroke 51"
NHP	402
Built by	Blair & Co., Ltd.
At	Stockton-on-Tees
History	

Disposal
1935, September 26: wrecked on Tregwin Rocks, Lizard Point, Cornwall, England.

Photo credit   Briscoe collection & Blackler collection

Name	**CLAN MACKENZIE (lll)**
Ex Names	
Official Number	137849
Signal letters	JQDF/GQMK
GRT as built	6544
NRT	4142
Dimensions in feet	420.1 x 53.4 x 36.2
Summer Draught	28' 2"
Built by	Northumberland Shipbuilding Co., Ltd.
Year	1917/6
At	Willington-upon-Tyne
Yard number	231
Engine type	T3 27", 44", 73" - Stroke 48"
NHP	662
Built by	North East Marine Engine Co., Ltd.
At	Newcastle-upon-Tyne

History

1918, March 3: torpedoed by a submarine off the Isle of Wight by a submarine, beached and later towed to Portsmouth, UK. 8 lives lost.

1937, October 23: beached in Liverpool Bay after a collision, declared a constructive total loss.

Disposal

1938: salved and broken up at Troon, Scotland.

Photo credit   Briscoe collection & Blackler collection

Name	**HARMODIUS (ll)**
Ex Names	**HERMIONE** - 1919
Official Number	140657
Signal letters	?/GCBX
GRT as built	5229
NRT	3179
Dimensions in feet	400.7 x 52.3 x 28.5
Summer Draught	25' 3½"
Built by	Ayrshire Dockyard Co., Ltd.
Year	1919/10
At	Irvine
Yard number	476
Engine type	T3 27", 44", 73" - Stroke 48"
NHP	517
Built by	Dunsmuir & Jackson Ltd.
At	Glasgow

History

1919: launched as **HERMIONE** for the Shipping Controller but handed over to Houston Line as **HARMODIUS**

Disposal

1941, March 8: torpedoed by a submarine, north-east of the Canary Islands, in Lat. 30° 35'N Long. 20° 40'W . The survivors were rescued by **HMS FAULKNOR** and landed at Gibraltar.

Photo credit   Briscoe collection.

Name	**CLAN MACMASTER**
Ex Names	**SUTHERLAND** - 1917
Official Number	140696
Signal letters	JQVP
GRT as built	6563
NRT	4137
Dimensions in feet	420.0 x 54.0 x 34.4
Summer Draught	28' 4"
Built by	Wm. Doxford & Sons Ltd.
Year	1917/8
At	Sunderland
Yard number	481
Engine type	T3 27", 44½", 75" - Stroke 54"
NHP	568
Built by	Richardsons Westgarth & Co., Ltd.
At	West Hartlepool

History

1917, December 24: launched for B. J. Sutherland & Co., Ltd., of Newcastle-upon-Tyne, as **SUTHERLAND**, and completed for Cayzer Irvine & Co., managers of Clan Line Steamers Ltd.

Disposal

1923: wrecked on Thousla Rock, Calf of Man, whist on a voyage from the Clyde, Scotland, to Liverpool, England.

Photo credit   Briscoe collection

Name	**CLAN MACBEAN (l)**
Ex Names	
Official Number	141876
Signal letters	JSKQ/GQMP
GRT as built	5052
NRT	3082
Dimensions in feet	400.0 x 52.4 x 28.0
Summer Draught	24' 10¼"
Built by	Bartram & Sons Ltd.
Year	1918/3
At	Sunderland
Yard number	243
Engine type	T3 27½", 45⅛", 75" - Stroke 48"
NHP	476
Built by	J. Dickinson & Sons Ltd.
At	Sunderland

History

1939: attacked by a torpedo and gunfire from a submarine. The torpedo missed and the **CLAN MACBEAN** attempted to ram the submarine which dived leaving its gun crew in the water.
One of the **CLAN MACBEAN**'s crew was lost overboard during the turning out of the lifeboats.
1947: sold to Goulandris Bros. (Okeanos Shipping Co.), Greece. Renamed **ANGLOS**.
1949: Renamed **KORTHION**.
1950: sold to Ubaldo Gennari fu Torquato, Pesaro, Italy. Renamed **AUDAX.**

Disposal

1959: arrived at Yawata, Japan, for breaking up.

Photo credit   Briscoe collection & Blackler collection (WSPL).

Name	**CLAN MORRISON**
Ex Names	
Official Number	141877
Signal letters	JSPV/GQMC
GRT as built	5931
NRT	3698
Dimensions in feet	409.6 x 53.5 x 33.5
Summer Draught	27' 9"
Built by	Ayrshire Dockyard Co., Ltd.
Year	1918
At	Irvine
Yard number	457
Engine type	T3 27½", 45½, 75" - Stroke 54"
NHP	413
Built by	Dunsmuir & Jackson Ltd.
At	Glasgow
History	

Disposal

1940, February 24: presumed to have hit a mine and sunk off the East Coast of England, 11 miles off Cromer Knoll lightvessel, in Lat. 53° 07'N Long. 1° 22'E. She was on a passage from Southampton, Hampshire, to Blyth, Northumberland. The Royal Navy rescued the crew who were landed at Grimsby, Lincolnshire.

Photo credit   Briscoe collection & Blackler collection

Officer Pinned Under Bridge

27/9/40

Ordeal On Sinking Ship In North Sea

When the 5,936-tons British steamer Clan Morrison struck a mine in the North Sea, Chief Officer Powell was trapped in the wreckage of the bridge, which was blown up by the explosion.

After half an hour's struggle the crew of the sinking vessel were able to extricate him. He was badly injured.

Second Officer Doyle, who led the rescue work, received slight injuries. A Lascar lost his life, and fifteen other Lascars were injured.

The vessel was still afloat when the crew took to three boats. They were picked up shortly afterwards, and were landed on Sunday at an East Coast port, where they were treated at hospital.

The Clan Morrison, which was owned by the Clan Line Steamers, Ltd., and which was built at Ayrshire in 1918, carried 15 officers under the command of Captain Hardinge, of Eastbourne. The crew were Lascars.—P.A.

Name	**CLAN MACVICAR**
Ex Names	**MAENWEN** – launched as
Official Number	141878
Signal letters	JSTP/GQMN
GRT as built	5815
NRT	3621
Dimensions in feet	400.1 x 53.0 x 32.8
Summer Draught	26' 2"
Built by	Northumberland Shipbuilding Co., Ltd.
Year	1918/3
At	Newcastle-upon-Tyne
Yard number	244
Engine type	T3 27", 45", 75" - Stroke 51"
NHP	569
Built by	North East Marine Engine Co., Ltd.
At	Newcastle-upon-Tyne

History

1917: launched as **MAENWEN** for W. & C. T. Jones S. S. Co. Ltd., Cardiff. Bought by Cayzer Irvine & Co. Ltd., during fitting out.

1936: sold to Counties Ship Management Co. Ltd., London and renamed **DOVER HILL**.

1942: on Russian convoys under J. & J. Denholm management.

Disposal

1944: sunk as a blockship at the Normandy Beaches, France.

Photo credit   Briscoe collection & Blackler collection (A. Duncan).

Name	**CLAN ALPINE (III)**
Ex Names	
Official Number	141879
Signal letters	JSTW/GQMR
GRT as built	6465
NRT	4762
Dimensions in feet	410.2 x 53.5 x 28.4
Summer Draught	26' 2"
Built by	Greenock & Grangemouth Dockyard Co. Ltd.
Year	1918/4
At	Greenock
Yard number	379
Engine type	T3 27", 44", 73" - Stroke 48"
NHP	538
Built by	J. G. Kincaid & Co. Ltd.
At	Greenock

History

1942: the Master was asked to evacuate 600 European women from Batavia but this was not done. In the event the ship loaded 977, mainly Asian, evacuees and took them to Ceylon and India.

Disposal

1943, March 13: sunk by escort after being damaged by a torpedo from a submarine, west of Cape Finisterre, Spain, in Lat. 42° 45'N Long. 13° 31'W. 26 crew were killed. 4 boats held 68 survivors who were picked up by **HMS SCARBOROUGH** 190 miles west of Cape Finisterre.

Photo credit   Briscoe collection & Blackler collection

Name	**CLAN MONROE (lll)**
Ex Names	
Official Number	141882
Signal letters	JTNK/GQMD
GRT as built	5919
NRT	3656
Dimensions in feet	409.6 x 53.4' x 33.5'
Summer Draught	26' 8"
Built by	Ayrshire Dockyard Co. Ltd.
Year	1918
At	Irvine
Yard number	466
Engine type	T3 27½", 45½", 75" - Stroke 54"
NHP	413
Built by	Dunsmuir & Jackson Ltd.
At	Glasgow
History	

Disposal

1940, July 29: sunk by a mine, in the Thames Estuary, Lat. 51° 52'N Long. 1° 48'E. Her cargo was 1,500 tons of manganese ore. 12 crew were killed.

Photo credit   Briscoe collection & Blackler collection (A. Duncan).

100

Name	**CLAN MACKINLAY (l)**
Ex Names	
Official Number	141890
Signal letters	JVSB/GQMT
GRT as built	6450
NRT	4135
Dimensions in feet	420.0 x 54.5 x 25.4
Summer Draught	27' 10"
Built by	W. Hamilton & Co. Ltd.
Year	1918/11
At	Port Glasgow
Yard number	308
Engine type	T3 29", 47", 78" - Stroke 54"
NHP	667
Built by	D. Rowan & Co. Ltd.
At	Glasgow
History	

Disposal

1940, November 16: bombed by aircraft. Sank, off the north-east coast of Scotland, in Lat. 58° 33'N, Long. 2° 53'W.

Photo credit   Briscoe collection & Blackler collection

**THE ALABAMA AFFAIR - The British Shipyards Conspiracy
in the American Civil War**
by David Hollett

This book reveals the turmoil and intrigue surrounding a deal involving the British government, the now defunct Merseyside shipyard of Cammell Laird and a country engaged in civil war, America.

· What was involved? · How was the conspiracy organised?
· Who were the shadowy figures at the centre of the controversy?
The Alabama Affair answers all the questions.
SBN 1 902964 04 7   £11.50 inc. p&p

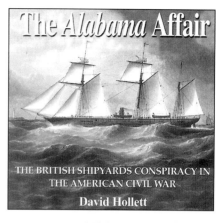

THE LIVERPOOL LIFEBOAT DISASTER OF 1892
One man's search for a missing piece of history -
by Jim Sullivan

'A labour of love that deserves to be told... a story of astonishing courage, brilliantly researched.' - Alan Bleasdale

ISBN   1 902964 10 1 £8.50 inc. p&p

LUSITANIA
by Colin Simpson

More than eighty years on the story of the Lusitania continues to be shrouded in mystery and suspicion. What was her real cargo? Why wasn't she protected? Why did she sink so quickly?
The Facts, the fictions, but most of all...the truth.

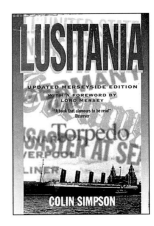

'A book that clamours to be read...' - The Observer
ISBN 0 9521020 6 4
£11.00 inc. p&p

THE FORGOTTEN EMPRESS - The Tragedy of the Empress of Ireland
By David Zeni

'...dubbed 'The 'Forgotten Empress'...the second in a shocking trio of tragedies at sea...sandwiched in between the disasters of the Titanic *and the* Lusitania, *...it was a sudden death... that sent Liverpool into mourning...'*
Liverpool Echo

ISBN 1 902964 15 2
£12.50 inc. p&p

THE GOLDEN WRECK - The Loss of the Royal Charter
By Alexander McKee

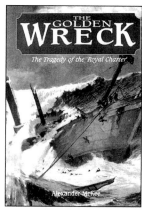

The effects great of the great hurricane of October 1859 were to shock the nation. 133 ships were sunk, 90 were badly damaged and almost 800 people lost their lives.

More than half of those that perished were on one ship - *The Royal Charter*.

The worst shipwreck in Welsh history, this is the story of the *Royal Charter*...and her gold.

ISBN 1 902964 0 2 0 £11.00 inc. p&p

IRON CLIPPER '*TAYLEUR*' – the White Star Line's 'First Titanic'
by H.F. Starkey

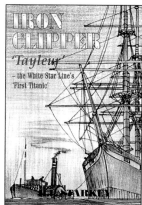

'Iron Clipper' is subtitled 'The First Titanic' for it tells the story of the first White Star liner to be lost on her maiden voyage. The '*Tayleur*' tragedy of 1854 and the '*Titanic*' catastrophe of 1912 are disasters which have so much in common that the many coincidences make this book appear to be a work which is stranger than fiction.

ISBN 1 902964 00 4

£8.00 inc. p&p

LIFE AT LAIRDS - Memories of working shipyard men
by David Roberts

When Cammell Lairds has gone and we are a generation or two down the line who will answer the questions 'What did they do there?' 'What was it like?' This book answers the questions.

- Sea Breezes

A Piece of Social History – Liverpool Echo

ISBN 0 9521020 1 3

£ 8.00 inc. p&p

{**Cammell Laird** - Old ships and Hardships: on Video. £14.99 inc. p&p in UK}

CAMMELL LAIRD - the golden years
by David Roberts.
Foreword by Frank Field MP

'Captures life in the prosperous years of the historic Birkenhead shipyard' - Liverpool Echo

'Puts into perspective...the strikes...the Polaris contract...and those who worked at the yard'

- Sea Breezes

ISBN 0 9521020 2 1

£7.50   inc. p&p

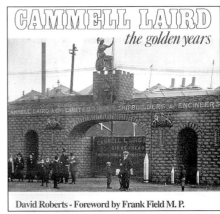

UNION - CASTLE - The Forgotten Navy
by Peter Abbott

Features the Intermediate liners, The Royal East Africa Service, Round Africa vessels, coasters, general cargo ships and reefers. Also covers the Zulu War, Boer War, World War I and World War II.

ISBN 1 902964 21 7 £11.00 inc. p&p

LUSITANIA AND BEYOND - the Life of Captain William Thomas Turner
by Mitch Peeke and Kevin Walsh Johnson

Over the years Captain Turner has been accused of treachery, stubbornness, ignorance and much worse. This book gives the true, remarkable story of Captain William Thomas Turner, the last Master of the doomed *Lusitania*.

ISBN 1 902964 14 4 £9.50 inc. p&p

A WELCOME IN THE HILLSIDES ?
- The Merseyside and North Wales Experience of Evacuation 1939 - 1945
by Jill Wallis

A book that is both informative and moving, with the real-life stories of the thousands of children who left the dangers of Merseyside for the safety of North Wales during World War II.

ISBN 1 902964 13 6 £12.00 inc. p&p

JUST NUISANCE AB - His full story
by Terence Sisson

The amazing but true story of the only dog that was officially enlisted into British Royal Navy, a Great Dane whose name was Nuisance, his official rank and name was AB Just Nuisance. Famed for his preference for the company of navy ratings (he wasn't too keen on Officers) in and around the famous World War II naval base of Simonstown, South Africa, Nuisance helped many a sailor rejoin his ship after a night on the town.   £8.00 inc. p&p

FROM BATTLEFIELD TO BLIGHTY
A History of Frodsham Auxiliary Hospital 1915-1919
by Arthur R Smith
The horrors of the first 'Great War' are well known, but the stories of those sent back from the 'Battlefield to Blighty' tend to be overlooked. This is the little known story in words and photographs of one of the largest auxiliary military hospitals in the country that was established at Frodsham in Cheshire during the First World War.
ISBN 1 9029640 16 0   £8.60 inc. p&p

FASTER THAN THE WIND - A History Guide to the Liverpool to Holyhead Telegraph.
by Frank Large
Take a journey along the one of most spectacular coastlines in Britain, the hills and countryside of North Wales and Wirral. The views are quite superb, and on a clear day it is possible to see just how signals about shipping were sent along the coast to and from Liverpool. This book contains full details of the intriguing and little known sites of the substantial remains of the Liverpool to Holyhead Telegraph Stations.
ISBN 0 9521020 9 9   £10.00 inc. p&p

TO ORDER BOOKS OR VIDEOS DIRECT CONTACT:-
Avid Publications, Garth Boulevard, Hr. Bebington, Wirral, Merseyside UK. CH63 5LS.
Tel / Fax 0151 645 2047
Look at the books and videos via the internet on
http://www.avidpublications.co.uk or E-mail info@AvidPublications.co.uk
Note. All prices here include postage and packaging within UK.